Snow Part

Schneepart

Other titles by Paul Celan
from Sheep Meadow Press

Fathomsuns and Benighted (2001)
    translated by Ian Fairley

Correspondence: Paul Celan and Nelly Sachs (1995)
    translated by Christopher Clark

Collected Prose (1990)
    translated by Rosmarie Waldrop

Snow Part

Schneepart

by Paul Celan

translated by Ian Fairley

The Sheep Meadow Press
Riverdale-on-Hudson, New York

All inquiries and permission requests should be addressed to:
The Sheep Meadow Press
P.O. Box 1345
Riverdale-on-Hudson, NY 10471

Designed and typeset by The Sheep Meadow Press.
Distributed by The University Press of New England.

Printed on acid-free paper in the United States. This book meets the guide-
lines for permanence and durability of the Committee on Production
Guidelines for Book Longevity of the Council on Library Resources.

Library of Congress Cataloging-in-Publication Data

Celan, Paul.
  [Schneepart. English & German]
  Snow part = Schneepart / by Paul Celan ; translated by Ian Fairley.
      p. cm.
  German and English.
  ISBN 1-931357-46-3
  I. Fairley, Ian, 1960- II. Title. III. Title: Snow part.

PT2605.E4S313 2006
831'.914--dc22
                                      2007001571

Acknowledgements

These translations have taken shape in conversation with Richard Ac-zel, Keith Bramall, Don Burbidge, Jenny Fairley, Stanley Moss, Bettina Schimmer and Jan Wallis, and in collaboration with Raymond Har-greaves. Steven Matthews, Anja Lemke and Saskia Reither gave me the opportunity to think about Celan in Oxford and in Frankfurt. I also wish to thank the editors of *Stand*, in which some of this work first appeared.

This book is for Jenny.

Contents

GEDICHTE AUS DEM
NACHLASS
(1968-1969)

OTHER POEMS
(1968-1969)

Introduction: *Iceland*

There was speech in their dumbness, language
in their very gesture; they look'd as they had
heard of a world ransom'd, or one destroy'd.

The Winter's Tale

The seventy poems which Paul Celan gathered in *Schneepart*
were written between December 1967 and October 1968. They stand
in the order of their composition. Celan presented the poems to his
wife in a manuscript dated 22 September 1969. A typescript bearing
the same date differs from this fair copy in some small details and
some more significant revisions. It is preceded by an epigraph, "Die
Welt ins Reine, Unabänderliche, Wahre heben" ("To raise the world
into the pure, immutable, true"), which adapts a diary entry by Franz
Kafka of 25 September 1917. On the joint authority of typescript
and manuscript, *Schneepart* was issued by Suhrkamp Verlag in 1971,
one year after its author drowned himself in the River Seine.

Celan did not authorize the publication of *Schneepart*, and
an instruction to the contrary, "Nicht veröffentlichen," attaches to
a draft title page for the collection. However the care which he de-
voted to its fair copy, which was issued in facsimile in 1976, is deemed
by the editors of the *Gesammelte Werke* (*Collected Works*, 1983) to be
consistent with Celan's practice in preparing earlier volumes and to
offer firm ground on which to infer his intention to publish. The
text of *Schneepart* which is reproduced in parallel with my translation
is that of the *Gesammelte Werke*. This departs from the first edition
solely in its version of the opening poem, "Ungewaschen, unbemalt"
("Unwashed, unprimed"), where the printer's insertion of "Ja" for
"da" ("Yes" for "there") in line four is corrected, and, in accord with
Celan's fair copy, the concluding full-stop is removed. "Ungewaschen,

unbemalt" is one of four poems which Celan sought to publish in advance of *Schneepart*: in 1968 he contributed what were to become the volume's first three poems, all written in Berlin, to *Hommage für Peter Huchel*, in honour of the leading East German (and East Berlin) poet; the fourth poem, "Ein Blatt, baumlos" ("A leaf, treeless"), was intended for a book of responses to Bertolt Brecht, *Von den Nachgeborenen* (*From the After-Born*, 1970).

Textual-critical editions recording the emergence of *Schneepart* as a volume and the compositional stages of its poems appeared in 1994 and 2002. Each is careful to not to claim an authorial last word for *Schneepart*, and to place it among Celan's *Nachlaß* or literary remains. Over sixty further poems exist from the volume's ten months of writing, two-thirds from July 1968, and one list of contents for *Schneepart* projects, before its revision, a total of ninety-nine titles. This work, among much else, was made accessible with the publication of Celan's *Gedichte aus dem Nachlaß* (*Uncollected Poems*) in 1997. Most of the "Other Poems" from 1968 and 1969 which supplement my translation are taken from this source; they comprise a chronological but in other respects heterogeneous sequence of poems both considered for or contemporary with *Schneepart* and written in its wake, the latest of which, "Kew Gardens," is from April 1969. The three epigrammatic pieces which conclude these "Other Poems" were set down in the summer of 1968, and are among the materials assembled in and documenting *Die Goll-Affäre* (*The Goll Affair*, 2000), the controversy generated by the accusation, first voiced in the 1950s, that Celan had plagiarized the poetry of Yvan Goll. My choices among this "uncollected" verse incline to aphorism and epigram, and are intended to pick up the voice of *Schneepart* and to let it carry.

The list of contents attaching to the fair copy which Celan gave to his wife extends only to the first poem, "Stahlschüßiger Sehstein" ("Steelshot lens-stone"), of the volume's fifth and final cycle, indicating that he may have been unsure of its make-up. That he considered certain of its poems for another project is suggested by an exercise book in which they keep the company of a group of pieces from the period August 1968 to January 1969 designated

"Nach Schneepart" ("After Schneepart"). In Celan's manuscript, the second poem in cycle five, "Und Kraft und Schmerz" ("And force and pain"), has a pencil line through the text and a question mark in one corner of the page. In the identical typescript he inks out one of its lines, "dein Typhus, Tanja," ("your typhus, Tanja,"), which would otherwise stand as a distinct verse paragraph between lines six and seven of the text given in the first edition of *Schneepart*, in the *Gesammelte Werke*, and in the present book. The second major difference between typescript and manuscript concerns another late poem, "Leuchtstäbe" ("Flashlights"), in which line fifteen of Celan's fair copy reads "dem Klöten-ZK" ("the ballocks-ZK"), but here, following the typescript cancellation observed by the 1971 and 1983 editions, is given as "dem ZK." (This acronym for *Zentralkomitee*, or Central Committee, is an inversion of *KZ: Konzentrationslager*, or concentration camp). Both excisions are restored in the single-volume annotated edition of Celan's complete poetry, *Die Gedichte* (*The Poems*, 2003), which has some claim to represent an alternative, if not preferred, authority to the *Gesammelte Werke*.

Celan's letters make a number of comments on individual poems and on *Schneepart* itself. To Franz Wurm, in January 1968, he sends a poem, "Was näht" ("What knits"), which strikes him as having "grown out of simple words": "entstanden, aus, wie mir auffällt, einfachen Worten." In July 1969 he gave Wurm, now living in Prague, "Kalk-Krokus" ("Chalk crocus"), written a year before in response to the Warsaw Pact invasion of Czechoslovakia, with the instruction to show it to the city "»wenn der Abend kommt«," the last words of Kafka's "A Message from the Emperor": "No one can force a way through here, least of all with a message from a dead man. But you sit by your window and dream it all true, when evening comes." To his wife, on 23 August 1968, Celan reports that he is face to face with the "problems of poetry" ("Les problèmes de la poésie se posent à moi avec une grande acuité") as events in Czechoslovakia press upon his writing ("me sollicitent au milieu de ce que j'écris, de ce que j'essaie d'écrire"). He then adds that he has been "rereading the poems written since *Fadensonnen*, now and then with the urge, the wish to reshape some of them," and that, for his most recent poems, he has "rediscovered... the compact diction [he] had been hoping to find. This will be a new book": "J'ai relu, assez souvent, les poèmes écrits depuis <Fadensonnen>, par moments avec la tentation, avec l'envie de mieux contourer certains d'entre eux. Il y a peu de jours, j'ai retrouvé, pour de nouveaux poèmes, la diction compacte que je souhaitais trouver. Ce sera un nouveau livre." These poems after *Fadensonnen* (*Fathomsuns*, 1968) are those composed since the middle of 1967 and collected in *Lichtzwang* (*Force of Light*, 1970), the last volume which Celan entrusted to his publisher before his death. His "new poems" ("Leuchtstäbe" is from two days before, and "Kalk-Krokus" from the day after, this letter) were to be collected in the "new book" *Schneepart*, although at the time they may have been intended for a new book *after Schneepart*. Writing in January 1970 to Ilana Shmueli, Celan announces that "der Band nach dem nächsten ist wohl das Stärkste, Kühnste, das ich geschrieben habe. (Geschrieben zwischen Dezember 67 und Oktober 68)": "the volume after next [that is, after *Lichtzwang*] is probably the strongest, the boldest that I've written. (Written between December 67 and October 68)."

   This is to sketch something of the circumstance of *Schneepart*. That *Schneepart* is a volume dark with circumstance has preoccupied much of the commentary devoted to its poetry. Perhaps the best known work to address this concern is Peter Szondi's "Eden," which annotates the sights, places and associations of "Du liegst" ("You lie"), written during Celan's visit to Berlin, where he met with Szondi and others, in December 1967: the "meathooks" which the poem's "you" is urged to witness ("geh zu den Fleischerhaken") are those on which the anti-Hitler Kreisau Group conspirators were hanged in 1944; the commandeered Hotel "Eden" was where Karl Liebknecht and Rosa Luxemburg, leaders of the 1919 Spartacist uprising, were imprisoned before they were shot, and Luxemburg's body thrown in Berlin's Landwehrkanal. In "Du liegst", a poem situated on the eve of Christmas, writer and reader are "hedged round, snowed round" ("umbuscht, umflockt') with violence. Other poems speak recognizably of uprising and state (para)military force in Paris and in Prague, while less recognizably, "Mapesbury Road," composed in London over Easter-Passover 1968, registers the attempted assassination of student leader Rudi Dutschke in Berlin, one week after the murder of Martin Luther King.

It is as if the condition of these poems – perhaps, the openness of these poems – lies in the recognition that circumstance is everywhere. Their synaptic density is one in which "reference" is most vitally a matter of Celan's re-articulation both of German speech and writing, and of Jewish-German memory and experience, making for a poetry which is at once dark and lucid, dark and legible. In the same moment, the motto that "circumstance is everywhere" can be taken as an index, in paraphrase, of the psychic crisis of and from which much of the poetry in *Schneepart* speaks. Most of the poems in the volume's typescript and fair copy are inscribed "Rue Tournefort," where, from November 1967, Celan lived apart from his family, at his wife's request, after leaving the psychiatric hospital in which he had been resident since his attempted suicide on 30 January – an action possibly prompted by a chance meeting with Yvan Goll's widow, identified by Celan as his chief persecutor. One of those poems, "Ein Leseast" ("A reading branch"), composed in late August 1968, moves from oblique recollection of this attempt on his life ("vorm / Blutklumpenort": "before the / bloodclot point") to a projection of and identification with Czech independence of mind: that of a "capital, not to / be seized," where the resistance to occupation described by the poem's closing "unbesetzbare" has to do with consciousness as much as country. Neither Soviet nor any other *Besetzung* (in Freudian translation, "cathexis") can hold sway for this "Meerstück," or stretch of littoral, which so recalls a "sea-coast of Bohemia."

In November 1968, however, one month after writing *Schneepart's* last poem, Celan again entered a psychiatric hospital following a further persecution-fraught incident. That among such distress – circumstance – his writing holds and bears reading is borne out by the uncannily emblematic movement of a poem from 1969, later published in *Zeitgehöft* (*Timestead*, 1976):

Es wird etwas sein, später,	There will be something, later,
das füllt sich mit dir	that fills with you
und hebt sich	and lifts itself
an einen Mund	to a mouth
Aus dem zerscherbten	I stand
Wahn	up from the shatter of
steh ich auf	madness
und seh meiner Hand zu,	and watch my hand
wie sie den einen	trace the one
einzigen	single
Kreis zieht	circle

The act of standing, of rising up, at the imaginative centre of Celan's poetry and of this poem, follows the shattering of a "madness" the terrible coherence of which is *zerscherbt*, in shards. The poet stands in mindful relation to a circle – which can be conceived, I suggest, as the circle of circumstance – and in internally distanced relation to himself, as if returned to a circuit of self-estrangement and self-recognition. His hand seems to have a mind of its own, and to know what it draws by heart. In the imperfect symmetry, created by the fact of standing, between the poem's last and first four lines, a gesture is delineated but is not – not even in the tracing of a unique circle – completed. The figure of this circle is made to stand, empty, and so to correspond, in a way yet to be decided, to the prediction of the first lines: it may stand for "something," for "you," and for "mouth"; and it can also stand for Celan's madness. The poem's gesture, its speech act, returns, through this "one" circle, from "I" to "you," or perhaps to an "I" now thinkable as both "you" and "I." It turns toward the thought of being filled by, or of filling, another.

      The line of this poem is akin to that of the "connective" ("das Verbindende") named in the title of Celan's speech *Der Meridian* (*The Meridian*, 1960), made upon receipt of the Georg Büchner Prize for Literature. Here the poet reports finding "something – like language – immaterial, yet earthly, terrestrial, something in the shape of a circle" which, through a process of self-essaying and self-prospecting ("ein Sichvorausschicken zu sich selbst"), describes the path "from a voice to a listening you" ("zu einem wahrnehmenden Du"), and so to "A kind of homecoming": "Eine Art Heimkehr." For the poem, as Celan projects it, "every thing and every person is a figure of this other [*eine Gestalt dieses Anderen*] toward which it bears." This is to propose that the poem's standing toward its circumstance is a matter of bearing another in mind. It is also to anticipate the "otherwiseness" of Celan's address to the "none other" of which he writes – as if standing elsewhere in its midst. And it is with regard to the singularity of this stance that I offer my translations to stand and fall without annotation beyond these introductory remarks. In such circumstance, I think that translation has to be enough.

Within *Schneepart*, "home" ground is identified with the literal "being in two" of despair or *Verzweiflung*. It is of this brokenness that Celan speaks in "Steinschlag" ("Rockfall"):

| Da sah ich einen, der log nicht, | I saw one there, who didn't lie, |
| heimstehn in seine Verzweiflung. | stand the ground of his brokenness. |

Again there is talk of standing, tenaciously so, for the accusative "in seine" signals a step into, or something like an elective confession of despair, in order to stand or stay at home there; Celan's invention seems to call upon a legal and archaic sense of *heimstehen* as either "to revert to" or, by right, "to belong to." The homecoming pictured in "Heimkehr," from *Sprachgitter* (*Speech-Grille*, 1959), opens with the words "Schneefall, dichter und dichter": "Snowfall, thicker and thicker." In this iteration, the poet, *Dichter*, and the activity of being a poet, *dichten*, materialize, and at the core of its dense association of snowfall and poetry is "*dich*," an agglomeration of "you" and "I." The poem presents to the eye a whiteness in which "invisible" things are painfully made out, among them "the sledtrack of what's lost" ("die Schlittenspur des Verlornen"), and, on each whited-out hill, an "I," slid into muteness, which has been recalled or "brought home to its today": "heimgeholt in sein Heute, / ein ins Stumme entglittenes Ich." This "I" is, in a form of reverse personification, identified as a wooden stake or "Pflock" – echoic of *Flocke*, or snowflake – to which "a feeling" ("ein Gefühl") fastens "its dove-, its snow- / coloured flag": "sein tauben-, sein schnee- / farbenes Fahnentuch festmacht." Snow is the ground of Celan's heraldry of desolation, and "I" is a figure or *Gestalt* against this ground: the "figure of another," dumb and expressive, a sign of life, and of death. The poem appears to speak in tension with a drift toward speechlessness and oblivion, expressing an horizon of what is lost – a *horizon kuklos*, or bounding circle – which embraces the lost "you-I" incorporated in "dichter." This is a poem in which the presence of loss comes home, marked by each hilltop post and apprehended in the contour and rupture of whiteness. A ground is broken. In *Schneepart* I have translated the figure of Celan's doubly cleaving speech by two words, "snow part."

In modern German, *Part* signifies either a musical part, for instrument or voice, or a part enacted as a role; its meaning is not "portion" or "piece." Celan's drafts of the volume's title poem indicate one or other of the word's present-day senses: "Den Schneepart spielen, gebäumt, bis zuletzt": "To play the snow-part, erect, to the last." In this version, "gebäumt" – literally, "risen up like a tree," but usually meaning "reared up," as on hind legs – would describe the player rather than the part. In the finished poem, however, there is just "Schneepart, gebäumt, bis zuletzt." Standing alone, this "snow part" can perhaps be read as a foreshortened articulation of *Schneepartikel*: of the part – the essential element – in the irreducible, indeclinable, (sub-)atomic *particula* of "snow particle." The abrupting enacted by "Schneepart," and replicated in "gebäumt," releases, among other connotations, the second principal (and already archaic) sense of *Part* given in Grimm's dictionary: that of a contesting party or faction. And as the German word comes from the Middle French, and thence from Latin *part-* and *pars*, so an understanding of fraction, division and adherence carries over, in "Schneepart," to matters of territory and region (*in partibus*), as also to the analytics of parsing, part-song, and the parts of speech.

The region notated in this title poem bears resemblance to limestone alp or to a terrain marked by composite glaciofluvial and karstic erosion. Its final word, "Kolk," which means "deep pool" in Low German, describes a pit formed by the bore of water, and can be translated by a number of geological terms – among them, "pothole" and "swallow-hole" – which name a shaft or hollow created by the mill-like vortex of pebbles on a riverbed, by the scour of karstic (limestone) solution, or by the action of glacial meltwater. In counterpoint to depthless dreams ("Flachträume"), sent uncannily singing over a frozen surface, the poet endeavours to "hew out the word- / shadows, to cord them / round the cramp-iron" in this deep place: "die Wortschatten / heraushaun, sie klaftern / rings um den Krampen / im Kolk." It is as if he excavates this pit in order to build within it: *klaftern* can mean both "to fathom" (to measure by outstretched arms) and "to cord," which is to stack wood cut to the measure of a cord or *Klafter*. This occupation seems to invert and repeat the schema of those huts, made untenantable or barely habitable by the loss of their windows, before which the poem's "snow part" stands or is pitched; the etymology of *Kolk* includes "eye-hole," whereas windowless huts are without any "wind-eye." Here the binding and biting of the cramp-iron (*Krampe*) continues the intention of a "snow part" which holds "to the last," or until it can be held no more. Adverbially, the poem is already *zuletzt*, an advance guard of last words, for its world is one in which being alive and being dead partake. In looking to build from freed "wordshadows," Celan is true to the phenomenology of the cave, where shadow is the real. "Kolk" is shaded by white, calcified *Kalk*, as a grave might be cloaked in lime, while syllabically it carries – in a sign of release? – toward the foreshadowed other world, associated by Celan with lost homeland, of *Kolchis*. The poet speaks, stands, in the abysmal, swallowing space of the "Kolk"; he works upon it, sounds it, makes it speak, creates an interruptive breathing space within it. Celan speaks as a shade, or from his shade, among shades. He takes the part of snow.

If, in *Schneepart*, poetic address is only shadowed by elegy, that is because, from the volume's first poem, underworld shades into overworld. "Ungewaschen, unbemalt" describes a body or bodies unwashed and unpainted, unreadied in any ritual fashion for passage to a "beyond" or *Jenseits*. The poem's "we" are, materially, of this earth ("Erdige") and atomized, turned to cloud or dust ("Zerwölkte"). Waiting their time in a "shafthouse" or *Kaue* (from Latin *cavea*) which places them at the mouth of a mine, they appear to have missed the opportunity of transport in the "Becherwerk" or chain of buckets which passes through them with its cargo of "Narren- / beinen": "fools' bones," that is, laughing- or funny-bones. Rather, they are absorbed by a "flight shadow" which "heals" them in ("heilt uns ein") and issues in the numinous, "ice-age near" vision of the poem's final paragraph. The matter of what this shadow attaches to is as undeterminable as that of whether its flight carries toward or beyond a "beyond." Just as we come after an ice age which is still with us, so in *Schneepart* we stand amid deathdealing catastrophe and cast shadows into its glare. Those expelled spell out their dust. This is the limestone-white world where, in "Erzflitter" ("Oreflashes"), "Verlorenes findet / in Karstwannen / Kargheit, Klarheit." Celan's phrasing enables "what is lost" to be read as either the subject or object of "findet": "In karst basins / what's lost finds / poverty, clarity"; or, alternatively, "poverty, clarity, / finds what is lost." What matters in each reading is that something is said to be found. What is lost is expressed, apprehended, or brought to mind in the unpossessible properties of this place. An horizon is given to abyss. In such an act – in its translation between what is and is not there – Celan's poetry stands its broken ground, breaks the compass of its circumstance, conceives an orientation, and gives us pause.

Peter Szondi observes a halting motion in the last line of "Du liegst": with "Nichts / stockt" – "Nothing / stops" – something, the poem, stops. I wish to propose that it is in the shock and involuntary pause effected by this and similar lines that the act of reading and of translating Celan begins. The arrest of "Nichts / stockt" can be gauged against one of Celan's aphorisms in *Gegenlicht* (*Backlight*, 1948): "»Alles fließt«: auch dieser Gedanke, und bringt er nicht alles wieder zum Stehen?" This sentence might be translated: "'All things are flowing': this thought also, and doesn't that bring everything to a standstill?" Its propositional-interrogative movement returns us to ourselves as thinking, predicating, finite subjects. The recognition that "auch dieser Gedanke [fließt]" seems to bracket thought with universal flowing, surrendering that thought to its own current; yet in the next moment a mindful "und bringt er nicht...?" steps out of the parenthesis of what's just been thought as if to contemplate in it something reified and mutable, something which exists to be thought – the *Da-sein* of what is lost, or no more. Some such process corresponds, I think, to Celan's claim in *Der Meridian* that, in order to endure or withstand ("um bestehen zu können"), the poem "unendingly calls and pulls itself back from its 'already-no-more' into its 'still-here'": "ruft und holt sich... aus seinem »Schon-nicht-mehr« in sein »Immer-noch« zurück."

Gegenlicht means "against the light" and suggests a subject seen in eclipse. To make out what is shadow against this light calls for a vision which throws its own light. This "counter-light" anticipates Celan's thinking in *Der Meridian* about a "counter-word" or "Gegenwort" spoken from human solidarity in the face of human eclipse. The "Stehen" of Celan's aphorism could be said to follow from the initial counter-word "auch." By counting "dieser Gedanke" into "Alles fließt," this "also" intercepts the would-be Heraclitan formula of Plato's *Cratylus* and prevents the "nothing remains" which otherwise (at least in some translations) completes the proposition "All things are flowing." Something remains, to be thought.

In asking after the fate of "Alles fließt," Celan interrupts – atomizes – the ineluctable. In putting the question of "everything at a standstill" he sets something in motion. The "counter-word" which he cites in *Der Meridian* is Lucile's "Es lebe der König!" ("Long live the King!"), the line which brings Büchner's *Danton's Death* to a close. These "thoughtful" words – the stage direction describes Lucile, before she speaks, as "sinnend" – are glossed by Celan as "an act of freedom" and "a step": "es ist ein Akt der Freiheit. Es ist ein Schritt." In their own contradiction of process and predication, the last lines of "Du liegst" recall other of Lucile's words, from the play's immediately preceding scene, which Celan marked in his copy of Büchner:

"Der Strom des Lebens müßte stocken, wenn nur der eine Tropfe verschüttet würde." Celan's three lines, "Der Landwehrkanal wird nicht rauschen. [*The Landwehrkanal will not make a sound.*] / Nichts / stockt," resonate with Lucile's "The river of life would surely stop if a single drop [of blood] were spilled." They translate, as if crossing life's river, another's horror and protest into an unfrozen speaking back to terror: a speaking of terror back into its places. The literalizing "Gegenwort" of both poem and aphorism – each proposes an actuality which brings figuration to a standstill – counters the undifferentiated *logos* of "all things" and the modality of a present or *Gegenwart* which stays for no one. Celan's poem makes a debacle of that present by counting in its own "still-here" with its "already-no-more." Aphorism, which combines *aph-*, "from", and *horizein*, "to separate, to set bounds to," is an horizon of definition on which we make out one thing from another. The poem aphorizes in order to hold on to that horizon and its prospect of encounter.

Perhaps each poem, like the sea-coast of Bohemia, is an horizon which effects a standstill? To read Celan's poetry is to wonder what to make of it. Asked after, our understanding may stall in its answer, but the possibility, like the necessity, of reading and translating nonetheless remains. Its ground is the disarticulation which occurs in the moment and impact of encounter, and which is described in Celan's *Gespräch im Gebirg* (*Conversation in the Mountains*, 1960). Two Jews, cousins, meet in a place of rock, water and ice; as they stand and speak, "the stick is silent, the stone is silent, and the silence is no silence, no word falls mute and no sentence, it is just a pause, a gap in words, a blank space, you see the syllables all standing around": "es schweigt der Stock, es schweigt der Stein, und das Schweigen ist kein Schweigen, kein Wort ist da verstummt und kein Satz, eine Pause ists bloß, eine Wortlücke ists, eine Leerstelle ists, du siehst alle Silben umherstehn." Words are beside themselves, parts of speech are intermitted, but this unintegrated speaking, this primary telling apart, is in the nature of their meeting in a place which speaks a language "without I and without You": "eine Sprache, je nun, ohne Ich und Du." This is a moment in which things are and are not themselves, where silence is no silence, "and July is no July": "der Juli ist kein Juli." It is in these circumstances that the poet finds a language, in this place that his words bear toward another – toward "you" and "I." How they do so is signalled among Celan's notes for *Der Meridian*: "Es gibt kein Wort, das, ausgesprochen, nicht den übertragenen Sinn mitbrächte: im Gedicht *meinen* die Worte unübertragbar zu sein." In other words, "in the poem, words *mean* to be untranslatable," yet "there is no word which, when spoken, will not contain its translated meaning." (Here "den übertragenen Sinn" and "unübertragbar" describe the "figurative" quality of the spoken word and the poem's "non-figurative" intention). The poetry of Celan challenges us to hold together the two parts of this statement, as if the poem's intention is to assert the non-identity of recognition and possessive knowing in the address of "I" to "you." To say "you" – a form of *meinen* which contains its Middle High German association with *Minne*, meaning "love" – instead makes for the release into alterity of both "I" and "you." The interlocutors of *Gespräch im Gebirg* each know what it is like to speak to no one, asking "Do you hear me?" ("Hörst du?"), but receiving no reply "because Do-you-hear-me is with the glaciers": "denn Hörstdu, das ist mit den Gletschern." The poet is the ventriloquist of the tongue-tied glacier. We are his audience.

The poem, says Celan, intends a "truly receiving you" ("einem wahrnehmenden Du"), one who listens rightly. In our reciprocal bearing toward the poem on its horizon, the reader and translator face, to paraphrase Martin Heidegger, one side of a surrounding openness – even, one side of an encircling abyss. To conclude, I should like to observe how stopping to listen to Celan is responsive both to the translatable and to the untranslatable intendedness of his verse. The first lines of "Mauerspruch" ("What the wall says") invite this recognition:

Entstellt – ein Engel, erneut, hört auf –
kommt ein Gesicht zu sich selber

Defaced – an angel, made new, elapses –
a vision discovers itself

The parenthesis after "Entstellt" ("Disfigured") reports an abrupt mutation: an angel, renewed, stops; ceases to be, perhaps. Yet "hört auf" contains its own double moment – one of stopping and listening – which enables us to hear consequence in the contiguity of "erneut, hört auf," and to enter the contradictory logic of a visage or vision ("Gesicht") said to come to itself ("kommt… zu sich selber") in its defacement. For the history of the verb *aufhören* involves a translation from hearing (*hören*) to stopping which the poem immediately translates back; as if an imperative *hört auf!* were to command us to stop what we're doing and "listen up," so an horizon of attention surfaces at the end of this initial line. Kluge's etymological dictionary offers a naturalistic gloss on the dialectic of *aufhören*, noting that we cease immediate activity whenever we direct our attention toward an object: "Wenn jemand auf etwas sein Augenmerk richtet, dann läßt er zugleich von seiner Tätigkeit ab." Discontinuing is one side of giving attention ("das Ablassen ist deshalb ein anderer Aspekt des Aufmerkens"), and from this follows the "translation" ("daher die Übertragung") from hearing to ceasing. The poem's astounding "bearing across" from ceasing (in)to hearing – an angel's *audit ad dominum*, or "hearing up" to God? – may be untranslatably material to Celan's German, but it remains to be listened for on translation's horizon. To hear it is to receive part of what the poem is open to in its circumstance. With this we are returned to the apprehension of "Du liegst im großen Gelausche": "You lie in the great listening." "Gelausche" is formed from the verb *lauschen*, which means "to listen intently," "to eavesdrop," or "to lie in wait for," and which rhymes with "Der Landwehrkanal wird nicht *rauschen*": "will not sound." The poet predicts the silencing – conceivably, the continued silence – of the canal, the swallowing of a sound, which can extend from a murmur to a roar, associated with the "com-motion" of wind and water, and also with poetry's ecstatic "rush." What we hear in this line is the sound of motion stilled, a *Rauschen* heard in different aspects throughout *Schneepart*, and not translated by the same word twice.

With my thanks to Don Burbidge.

Ian Fairley, 2007

Texts by and about Paul Celan cited or quoted

The place of publication and publisher are, unless otherwise noted, Frankfurt am Main and Suhrkamp Verlag.

By Paul Celan

• Poetry

Schneepart (1971).

Schneepart: Faksimile der Handschrift aus dem Nachlaß (1976).

Gesammelte Werke, Volume II, *Atemwende, Fadensonnen, Lichtzwang, Schneepart*, ed. Beda Alleman and Stefan Reichert with Rolf Bücher (5 vols, 1983).

Schneepart, ed. Rolf Bücher with Axel Gellhaus and Andreas Lohr-Jasperneite (*Werke*, Historisch-kritische Ausgabe, vols 10.1 and 10.2; 1994).

Die Gedichte aus dem Nachlaß, ed. Bertrand Badiou, Jean-Claude Rambach and Barbara Wiedemann (1997).

Schneepart: Vorstufen – Textgenese – Reinschrift, ed. Heino Schmull with Markus Heilman (*Werke*, Tübinger Ausgabe; 2002).

Die Gedichte: Kommentierte Gesamtausgabe in einem Band, ed. Barbara Wiedemann (2003).

• Prose

Gesammelte Werke, Volume III, *Gedichte III, Prosa, Reden*, ed. Beda Al-
leman and Stefan Reichert with Rolf Bücher (5 vols, 1983).

Collected Prose, trans. Rosmarie Waldrop (Riverdale: Sheep Meadow
Press, 1990).

Der Meridian: Endfassung – Entwürfe – Materialien, ed. Berhard
Böschenstein and Heino Schmull with Michael Schwarz-
kopf and Christiane Wittkop (*Werke*, Tübinger Ausgabe;
1999).

• Correspondence

Paul Celan and Franz Wurm, *Briefwechsel*, ed. Barbara Wiedemann
with Franz Wurm (1995).

Paul Celan and Gisèle Celan-Lestrange, *Correspondance (1951-1970)*:
Avec un choix de lettres de Paul Celan à son fils Eric,
ed. Bertrand Badiou with Eric Celan (2 vols, Paris: Éditions
du Seuil, 2001).

Paul Celan and Ilana Shmueli, *Briefwechsel*, ed. Ilana Shmueli and
Thomas Sparr (2004).

On Paul Celan

Peter Szondi, *Celan Studies*, trans. Susan Bernofsky and Harvey
Mendelsohn (Stanford, CA: Stanford University Press, 2003).

Barbara Wiedemann, ed., *Paul Celan – Die Goll-Affäre: Dokumente
zu einer ›Infamie‹* (2000).

Snow Part

Schneepart

I

UNGEWASCHEN, UNBEMALT,
in der Jenseits-
Kaue:

da,
wo wir uns finden,
Erdige, immer,

ein
verspätetes
Becherwerk geht
durch uns Zerwölkte hindurch,
nach oben, nach unten,

aufrührerisch
flötets darin, mit Narren-
beinen,

der Flugschatten im
irisierenden Rund
heilt uns ein, in der Sieben-
höhe,

eiszeitlich nah
steuert das Filzschwanenpaar
durch die schwebende
Stein-Ikone

Unwashed, unprimed,
in the afterworld
shafthouse:

there,
where we find ourselves,
claybound, ever,

a
late-running
bucket chain winds
through us, cloudshot,
on its way up, down,

unruly
whistling inside, with laughing-
bones,

the flight shadow in
the iridescent round
incarns us in the seventh
height,

ice-age near
two swans of felt
steer through the hovering
stone-icon

DU LIEGST im großen Gelausche,
umbuscht, umflockt.

Geh du zur Spree, geh zur Havel,
geh zu den Fleischerhaken,
zu den roten Äppelstaken
aus Schweden –

Es kommt der Tisch mit den Gaben,
er biegt um ein Eden –

Der Mann ward zum Sieb, die Frau
mußte schwimmen, die Sau,
für sich, für keinen, für jeden –

Der Landwehrkanal wird nicht rauschen.
Nichts
        stockt.

YOU LIE in the great auricle,
groved round, snowed round.

Go to the Spree, go to the Havel,
go to the butchers' hooks,
to the red impaled apples
from Sweden –

The table of gifts draws near,
it turns round an Eden –

The man was made sieve, the woman
had to swim, the sow,
for herself, for no one, for everyone –

The Landwehrkanal won't sound.
Nothing's
        still.

LILA LUFT mit gelben Fensterflecken,

der Jakobsstab überm
Anhalter Trumm,

Kokelstunde, noch nichts
Interkurrierendes,

von der
Stehkneipe zur
Schneekneipe.

LILAC SKY, yellow paned,

Jacob's Staff above the
Terminus wreck,

lighting-up time, as yet
nothing intercurrent,

from
stand-up bar to
snow bar.

BRUNNENGRÄBER im Wind:

es wird einer die Bratsche spielen, tagabwärts, im Krug,
es wird einer kopfstehn im Wort Genug,
es wird einer kreuzbeinig hängen im Tor, bei der Winde.

Dies Jahr
rauscht nicht hinüber,
es stürzt den Dezember zurück, den November,
es gräbt seine Wunden um,
es öffnet sich dir, junger
Gräber-
brunnen,
Zwölfmund.

WELL-GRAVERS in the wind:

one will play fiddle, as day dwindles, in the inn,
one will stand on his head in the word Enough,
one will hang crosslegged in the weedbound gate.

This year
won't blow over,
it bowls back December, November,
it unearths its wounds,
it opens to you, young
grave-
well,
twelvemouth.

DAS ANGEBROCHENE JAHR
mit dem modernden Kanten
Wahnbrot.

Trink
aus meinem Mund.

THE BREACHED YEAR
with its mouldering crust
of lunebread.

Drink
from my mouth.

UNLESBARKEIT dieser
Welt. Alles doppelt.

Die starken Uhren
geben der Spaltstunde recht,
heiser.

Du, in dein Tiefstes geklemmt,
entsteigst dir
für immer.

UNREADABLE this
world. All doubles.

Strong clocks
accord the cleft hour
hoarsely.

You, clamped in your deepest,
climb out of yourself
for ever.

HURIGES SONST. Und die Ewigkeit
blutschwarz umbabelt.

Vermurt
von deinen lehmigen Locken
mein Glaube.

Zwei Finger, handfern,
errudern den moorigen
Schwur.

WHORISH THEN. And eternity,
babeled round bloodblack.

Mired
by your claggy locks
my faith.

Two fingers, hand-far,
row the grimpen
oath.

WAS NÄHT
an dieser Stimme? Woran
näht diese
Stimme
diesseits, jenseits?

Die Abgründe sind
eingeschworen auf Weiß, ihnen
entstieg
die Schneenadel,

schluck sie,

du ordnest die Welt,
das zählt
soviel wie neun Namen,
auf Knien genannt,

Tumuli, Tumuli,
du
hügelst hinweg, lebendig,
komm
in den Kuß,

ein Flossenschlag,
stet,
lichtet die Buchten,
du gehst
vor Anker, dein Schatten
streift dich ab im Gebüsch,

Ankunft,
Abkunft,

WHAT KNITS
at this voice? At what
does this voice
knit
on this side and on that?

The chasms are
sworn to white, from them
sprang
the snow needle,

swallow it,

you order the world,
in sum
a good nine names,
named kneeling,

tumuli, tumuli,
you
hill out of there, alive,
come
into the kiss,

a steady
finbeat
clears the bays,
you drop
anchor, your shadow
strips you off in the scrub,

arrival,
origin,

ein Käfer erkennt dich,
ihr steht euch
bevor,
Raupen
spinnen euch ein,

die Große
Kugel
gewährt euch den Durchzug,

bald
knüpft das Blatt seine Ader an deine,
Funken
müssen hindurch,
eine Atemnot lang,

es steht dir ein Baum zu, ein Tag,
er entziffert die Zahl,

ein Wort, mit all seinem Grün,
geht in sich, verpflanzt sich,

folg ihm

a beetle knows you,
you verge on
yourselves,
worms
inweb you,

the great
globe
accords you both safe passage,

soon
the leaf knots its vein to yours,
sparks
must through,
in a stopping of the breath,

there's a tree, a day, that stands as yours,
it deciphers the number,

a word, with all its green,
turns within, transplants itself,

follow it

ICH HÖRE, DIE AXT HAT GEBLÜHT,
ich höre, der Ort ist nicht nennbar,

ich höre, das Brot, das ihn ansieht,
heilt den Erhängten,
das Brot, das ihn die Frau buk,

ich höre, sie nennen das Leben
die einzige Zuflucht.

I HEAR THE AXE HAS FLOWERED,
I hear the place can't be named,

I hear the bread that looks on him
heals the hanged man,
the bread his wife baked him,

I hear they call life
the only refuge.

MIT DER STIMME DER FELDMAUS
quiekst du herauf,

eine scharfe
Klammer,
beißt du dich mir durchs Hemd in die Haut,

ein Tuch,
gleitest du mir auf den Mund,
mitten in meiner
dich Schatten beschwerenden
Rede.

WITH A FIELDMOUSE VOICE
you squeak up,

a sharp
clamp,
you bite through my vest into flesh,

a cloth,
you slip over my mouth,
even as my talk
would weigh you, shadow,
down.

IN ECHSEN-
häute, Fall-
süchtige,
bett ich dich, auf den Simsen,
die Giebel-
löcher
schütten uns zu, mit Lichtdung.

IN LIZARD
skins, Epi-
leptic,
I bed you, on the sills,
the gable
holes
infill us, with lightsoil.

SCHNEEPART, gebäumt, bis zuletzt,
im Aufwind, vor
den für immer entfensterten
Hütten:

Flachträume schirken
übers
geriffelte Eis;

die Wortschatten
heraushaun, sie klaftern
rings um den Krampen
im Kolk.

SNOW PART, pitched, to the last,
in the updraught, before
for ever unwindowed
huts:

to skim flat dreams
over
fretted ice;

to hew out the word-
shadows, to cord them
round the cramp-iron
in the pit.

II

DIE NACHZUSTOTTERNDE WELT
bei der ich zu Gast
gewesen sein werde, ein Name,
herabgeschwitzt von der Mauer,
an der eine Wunde hochleckt.

THE WORLD TO BE STAMMERED AFTER
in which I'll have
been guest, a name,
sweated down from the wall
up which a wound licks.

DU MIT DER FINSTERZWILLE,
du mit dem Stein:

Es ist Überabend,
ich leuchte hinter mir selbst.
Hol mich runter,
mach mit uns
Ernst.

YOU WITH THE DARK SLING,
you with the stone:

It is the night's night,
I shine behind me.
Bring me down,
take us for
real.

EINGEJÄNNERT
in der bedornten
Balme. (Betrink dich
und nenn sie
Paris.)

Frostgesiegelt die Schulter;
stille
Schuttkäuze drauf;
Buchstaben zwischen den Zehen;
Gewißheit.

JANUARIED
in the thorned rock-
shelter. (Get drunk
and call it
Paris.)

My frostsealed shoulder;
on it
mute scree-owls;
runes between toes;
certainty.

SCHLUDERE, Schmerz,
schlag ihr nicht ins Gesicht,
erpfusch dir
die Sandknubbe im
weißen Daneben.

FOUL UP, pain,
spare her face,
make your mess
the sandknot in the
white amiss.

STÜCKGUT gebacken,
groschengroß, aus
überständigem Licht;

Verzweiflung hinzugeschippt,
Streugut;

ins Gleis gehoben, die volle
Schattenrad-Lore.

PARCEL FREIGHT, baked
groatbig from
unfelled light;

despair shovelled in,
aggregate;

winched onto tracks, the laden
shadow-wheel wagon.

VON QUERAB
komm ein, als die Nacht,
das Notsegel
bauscht sich,

eingeschreint
an Bord
ist dein Schrei,
du warst da, du bist unten,

unterhalb bist du,

ich geh, ich geh mit den Fingern
von mir,
dich zu sehn,
mit den Fingern, du Untre,

die Armstrünke wuchern,

das Leuchtfeuer denkt
für den ein-
sternigen Himmel,

mit dem Schwertkiel
les ich dich auf.

PUT IN
abeam, as the night,
juryrig
billowing,

your cry is
inshrined
on board,
you were there, you are below,

you are there below,

I go, I go with my fingers
out
to see you,
with my fingers, woman below,

armtrunks multiply,

the beacon thinks
for the one-
starred heavens,

with my drop-keel
I pick you up.

HOLZGESICHTIGER,
schlackermäuliger
Narr überm Tretrad:

am Ohrlappen hängt
dir das Aug
und hüpft
begrünt.

WOODENVISAGED,
slobbermouthed
fool over the treadwheel:

your eye hangs
by an earlobe
and hops
begreened.

LARGO

Gleichsinnige du, heidegängerisch Nahe:

über-
sterbens-
groß liegen
wir beieinander, die Zeit-
lose wimmelt
dir unter den atmenden Lidern,

das Amselpaar hängt
neben uns, unter
unsern gemeinsam droben mit-
ziehenden weißen

Meta-
stasen.

LARGO

Sameways you, heathfaring near one:

larger
than
death we lie
together, the autumn
crocus swarms
under your breathing lids,

the ouzel pair hang
beside us, under
the height of our white, fellow-
travelling

meta-
stases.

ZUR NACHTORDNUNG Über-
gerittener, Über-
geschlitterter, Über-
gewitterter,

Un-
besungener, Un-
bezwungener, Un-
umwundener, vor
die Irrenzelte gepflanzter

seelenbärtiger, hagel-
äugiger, Weißkies-
stotterer.

TO THE ORDER OF NIGHT Over-
ridden, Over-
slidden, Over-
swithined,

Un-
sung, Un-
swung, Un-
witherwrung,
planted ahead the bedlam tents,

soulbearded, hailstone-
eyed, Whitepebble-
stutterer.

MIT DEN SACKGASSEN sprechen
vom Gegenüber,
von seiner
expatriierten
Bedeutung –:

dieses
Brot kauen, mit
Schreibzähnen.

TO SPEAK with blind alleys
about what's facing,
about its
expatriate
sense —:

to chew this
bread, with
writing teeth.

ETWAS WIE NACHT, scharf-
züngiger als
gestern, als morgen;

etwas wie einer
Fischmäuligen Gruß
übern Jammer-
tresen;

etwas Zusammengewehtes
in Kinderfäusten;

etwas aus meinem
und keinerlei Stoff.

SOMETHING LIKE NIGHT, sharper
tongued than
yesterday, than tomorrow;

something like her
fishmouthed hello
over the counter
of woe;

something spindrift in
infant fists;

something made of my
and no matter.

III

WARUM DIESES JÄHE ZUHAUSE, mittenaus, mittenein?
Ich kann mich, schau, in dich senken, gletschrig,
du selbst erschlägst deine Brüder:
eher als sie
war ich bei dir, Geschneete.

Wirf deine Tropen
zum Rest:
einer will wissen,
warum ich bei Gott
nicht anders war als bei dir,

einer
will drin ersaufen,
zwei Bücher an Stelle der Lungen,

einer, der sich in dich stach,
beatmet den Stich,

einer, er war dir der nächste,
geht sich verloren,

einer schmückt dein Geschlecht
mit deinem und seinem Verrat,

vielleicht
war ich jeder

WHY SO ALL AT ONCE AT HOME, outmidst, inmidst?
Look, I can sink myself in you, glacial.
With your own hand you slay your brothers:
woman of snow, I was with you
before them.

Throw your tropes
to the rest:
someone wants to know
why I was no other with god
than with you,

someone
wants to drown in there,
two books in place of lungs,

someone who stabbed himself in you
gives mouth to the wound,

someone, he was nearest you,
loses himself,

someone gilds your sex
with your betrayal and his own,

perhaps
each one was me

WARUM AUS DEM UNGESCHÖPFTEN,
da's dich erwartet, am Ende, wieder
hinausstehn? Warum,
Sekundengläubiger, dieser
Wahnsold?

Metallwuchs, Seelenwuchs, Nichtswuchs.
Merkurius als Christ,
ein Weisensteinchen, flußaufwärts,
die Zeichen zuschanden-
gedeutet,

verkohlt, gefault, gewässert,

unoffenbarte, gewisse
Magnalia.

WHY STAND OUT, again,
of the uncreated, when
it expects you in the end?
Believer in seconds, why
these wages of folly?

Metal growth, soul growth, nothing growth.
Mercurius as Christ,
a philosopher's pebble, upstream,
the signs interpreted
to death,

charred, rotted, watered,

unrevealed, infallible
magnalia.

MAPESBURY ROAD

Die dir zugewinkte
Stille von hinterm
Schritt einer Schwarzen.

Ihr zur Seite
die
magnolienstündige Halbuhr
vor einem Rot,
das auch anderswo Sinn sucht –
oder auch nirgends.

Der volle
Zeithof um
einen Steckschuß, daneben, hirnig.

Die scharfgehimmelten höfigen
Schlucke Mitluft.

Vertag dich nicht, du.

MAPESBURY ROAD

The stillness flashed
at you from a black
woman's heel.

By her side
the
magnolia-houred halfclock
before a red that
also seeks meaning elsewhere –
or also nowhere.

The whole
court of time round
a lodged bullet, adjacent, cranial.

Sharply vaulted, curial gulps of
confluent air.

Now don't you adjourn.

DER ÜBERKÜBELTE ZURUF: dein
Gefährte, nennbar,
neben dem abgestoßenen Buchrand:

komm mit dem Leseschimmer,
es ist
die Barrikade.

THE OVERVAULTED CALL: your
helpmate, he can be named,
next to the chipped book-edge:

come with your reading shimmer,
this is
the barricade.

HERVORGEDUNKELT, noch einmal,
kommt deine Rede
zum vorgeschatteten Blatt-Trieb
der Buche.

Es ist
nichts herzumachen von euch,
du trägst eine Fremdheit zu Lehen.

Unendlich
hör ich den Stein in dir stehn.

ADUMBRATED, again,
your words succeed
to the beech's foreshadowed
leaf-sprit.

There is
none of you comes across,
you hold a strangeness in fee.

Endless,
I hear the stone in you stand.

MIT DIR DOCKE kungeln, es kommt
der Lumpenkarren daher-
gejazzt, mit uns
wills dahin,

die gestopfte
Trompete
haucht uns zeitauf,
ins härteste
Ohr dieser Welt,

auch so
klemmts uns Rot-
holzige zwischen
Zulieb und Zuleid,

dann,
wenn es uns loshakt,
sackst du mir mitten
ins Sein.

TO MONGER with you
doll, the ragcart comes
jazz-drawn, we will
be gone,

the stopped
trumpet
gasps us time-upward
into this world's most
hammered ear,

so too
are we red-
wood-clamped between
ill will and good,

then,
when we're unclipped,
you crease into my being's
middle.

AUCH DER RUNIGE wechselt die Fahrbahn:
mitten
im Greiftrupp
schabt er
sich Greifend-Gegriffenen rot,

Mohrrübe, Schwester,
mit deinen Schalen
pflanz mich Moorigen los
aus seinem
Morgen,

in den
Hochkörben, beim
abgerufenen Zündschwamm,
hinauf-
gestiegen ins phallische
Hirntransplantat, übertagt
der für immer geheutigte
Wundstein.

THE MAN OF RUNES, he too switches track:
at the centre
of the snatch squad he
scrapes himself,
snatching-snatched, red,

carrot, sister,
with your peel
plant me, moorbody,
free of his
tomorrow,

in tall
baskets, among
the repealed punkwood,
ascended
into the phallic head-
transplant, over-dayed,
the forever diurnal
elixir.

DEINEM, AUCH DEINEM
fehldurchläuteten Schatten
gab ich die Chance,

ihn, auch ihn
besteinigt ich mit mir
Gradgeschattetem, Grad-
geläutetem – ein
Sechsstern,
dem du dich hinschwiegst,

heute
schweig dich, wohin du magst,

Zeitunterheiligtes schleudernd,
längst, auch ich, auf der Straße,
tret ich, kein Herz zu empfangen,
zu mir ins Steinig-Viele
hinaus.

I GAVE A CHANCE
to your, even your
ill-rung shadow,

I bestoned
it, even it, with what's
true-shadowed, true-
rung of mine – a
six-pointed star
to which you gave your silence,

today
take your silence where you will,

strewing things timeunderhallowed,
long enough, I too, in the street,
I am bound, no heart to embrace,
for home, out into
the stony many.

MAUERSPRUCH

Entstellt – ein Engel, erneut, hört auf –
kommt ein Gesicht zu sich selber,

die Astral-
waffe mit
dem Gedächtnisschaft:
aufmerksam grüßt sie
ihre
denkenden Löwen.

WHAT THE WALL SAYS

Defaced – an angel, made new, elapses –
a vision discovers itself,

the astral
weapon with
the stock of memory:
intent, it salutes
its
mindful lions.

FÜR ERIC

Erleuchtet
rammt ein Gewissen
die hüben und drüben
gepestete Gleichung,

später als früh: früher
hält die Zeit sich die jähe
rebellische Waage,

ganz wie du, Sohn,
meine mit dir pfeilende
Hand.

FOR ERIC

A conscience,
enlightened, rams
the equation plagued
on both sides,

later than soon: time
sooner holds its sheer
rebellious balance,

just as you, son,
my hand that arrows
with you.

WER PFLÜGT NICHTS UM?
Er. Diesmal.
Unverackert
steht sein Land in den Sinn seiner Sonnen-
nächte.
Er nennt uns.

Ja, er kätnert.
Ja, er heißt gut, er belehmigt,
was du verhüttest
vor Ort,
hinter Ort,
über Ort, brach,
gegen die Erze,
zuunterst,
lebendig.

WHO BREAKS NO GROUND?
He. This time.
Untilled,
his land takes pattern at his solar
nights.
He names us.

Yes, he cottars.
Yes, he approves, he beloams
what you smelt
at the face,
behind the face,
over it, set-aside,
against the ores,
undermost,
quick.

LEVKOJEN, katzenbemündigt.
Beweibt
rechts von dir dieser Rasen.

Stab- und Mondsichel-Patt.

Du sollst nicht, so, gleich dir, hinterm Gitter, damals,
der
maltesische Jude, groß-
lippig – ihn
sprang der Knochen an, jäher
als dich, der Knochen,
den ein schon Morgiger warf –,
du
sollst nicht
aufsehn zum Himmel, du ließest
ihn denn, wie er dich,
im Stich, neben-
lichtig.
.   .   .   .
Schwester Kastanie, Vielblatt,
mit deinem blanken
Hiedrüben.

LEUCOJUMS, catfledged.
Wived
to the right of you, this grass.

Sickle-staff and -moon stalemate.

Thou shalt not, as like you, behind the grate, then,
the Malta-
Jew, thick-lipped –
the bone
leapt at him, suddener
than you, the bone
flung by a man already tomorrow's –,
thou
shalt not
look heavenward, or you leave
him, as he you,
in straits, aside-
light.
.   .   .   .
Sister chestnut, manyleaf,
with your incandent
hereyonder.

DU DURCHKLAFTERST
Farbenstoß, Zahlwurf, Verkenntnis,

viele
sagen:
du bists, wir verwissens,
viele verneinen sich an dir,
der du sie dir einzeln
erjast,
aufständisch wie
der dem Handgesagten geschenkte
Steinmut,
der sich hinhob zur Welt
am Saum des gewendeten Schweigens
und aller Gefahr.

YOU CORD THROUGH
bruising colour, spinning number, unkenning,

many
say:
it is you, don't we know it,
many deny themselves in you,
you who affirm them singly
to yourself,
risen up like the
stone courage
given him hand–spoken
who rose to meet the world
on the lip of turned silence and
every threat.

FÜR ERIC

In der Flüstertüte
buddelt Geschichte,

in den Vororten raupen die Tanks,

unser Glas
füllt sich mit Seide,

wir stehn.

FOR ERIC

History grubs
in the megaphone,

tanks worm the suburbs,

our glass
fills with silk,

we stand.

DEIN BLONDSCHATTEN, auf
Schwimmtrense gezäumt,
schwenkt die Wasserschabracke,

– auch du
hättest ein Recht auf Paris,
würdest du deiner
bitterer inne –,

dein Hankenmal, farblos
skizziert es die halb-
nahe Levade.

YOUR BLOND SHADOW, curbed
to the swimming-bit,
flashes its watershabrack,

– you too
would have a right to Paris
could you know yourself
more bitterly –,

the mark on your haunch
sketches, colourless, the half-
nigh levade.

DIE ABGRÜNDE STREUNEN: Summkies −:

dem kommst du bei
mit Taubheitsgefühlen
und Unschlaf,

und kämen − die Lockstoffe geistern
den Fahnenmast hoch −,
kämen auch hier
die Albembleme geflattert,
du wärst, dich erplündernd,
gebieterisch-gleich
ihr Entzwei.

ABYSMS prowl: huzzing gravel –:

you come at it
with numbness
and unsleeping,

and should – civet spirits
the flagstaff high –,
should here too
the alp-emblems come flying,
you were, your own reaver,
imperious-indifferent,
their in-two.

DEIN MÄHNEN-ECHO
– ihm wusch ich den Stein aus –,
mit Rauhreif beschlagen,
mit entsiegelter
Stirn beleu-
mundet
von mir.

THE ECHO OF YOUR MANE
– I washed out its stone –,
clad with rime,
with unsealed
brow re-
nowned
by me.

IV

DAS IM-OHRGERÄT treibt eine Blüte,
du bist ihr Jahr, dich beredet
die Welt ohne Zunge,
das weiß
jeder sechste.

THE DEVICE IN YOUR EAR unfurls
a blossom, you are its year,
the tongueless world talks
you round, one in six
knows it.

DER HALBZERFRESSENE Wimpel
frißt alle Länder vom Meer fort,
alle Meere vom Land,

ein weiterer Name
– du, du beleb dich! –
muß ein Ziffer
dulden,

Unzählbarer du:
um ein Un-
zeichen
bist du ihnen allen
voraus.

THE HALF-EATEN pennon
eats away all lands from the sea,
all seas from the land,

a further name
– you there, raise yourself! –
must endure a
number,

innumerable you:
by a mark that's
none
you steal a march
on them all.

EIN BLATT, baumlos,
für Bertolt Brecht:

Was sind das für Zeiten,
wo ein Gespräch
beinah ein Verbrechen ist,
weil es soviel Gesagtes
mit einschließt?

A LEAF, treeless,
for Bertolt Brecht:

What times are these
when conversation
amounts to a crime
for taking in so much
that is said?

PLAYTIME: die Fenster, auch sie,
lesen dir alles Geheime
heraus aus den Wirbeln
und spiegelns
ins gallertäugige Drüben,

doch
auch hier,
wo du die Farbe verfehlst, schert ein Mensch aus, entstummt,
wo die Zahl dich zu äffen versucht,
ballt sich Atem, dir zu,

gestärkt
hält die Stunde inne bei dir,
du sprichst,
du stehst,
den vergleichnisten Boten
aufs härteste über
an Stimme
an Stoff.

PLAYTIME: the windows, they too
read you what's ciphered
out of the swirling
and mirror it
into the jellyeyed beyond,

but
here too,
where you are blind to the colour, a man sheers out, unmuted,
where you are aped by the number,
breath concentrates, on you,

the fortified hour halts
with you,
you speak,
you stand,
hardmost above
the parabled messengers
in voice
in matter.

AUS DER VERGÄNGNIS
stehen die Stufen,

das ins Ohr Geträufelte
mündigt die Vorzeit darin,

Fjorde
sind Dochte,

nüchtern Erzähltes
träumt,

du berührst es, ein Tag-
verschworner.

THE STEPS CLIMB
out of mutability,

words dribbled in the ear
mature the foretime within,

fjords
are wicks,

the plain tale
dreams,

you touch on it, in league
with day.

OFFENE GLOTTIS, Luftstrom,
der
Vokal, wirksam,
mit dem einen
Formanten,

Mitlautstöße, gefiltert
von weithin
Ersichtlichem,

Reizschutz: Bewußtsein,

unbesetzbar
ich und auch du,

überwahr-
heitet
das augen-, das
gedächtnisgierige rollende
Waren-
zeichen,

der Schläfenlappen intakt,
wie der Sehstamm.

OPEN GLOTTIS, air stream,
the
vowel, active,
with the one
formant,

consonant clashes, filtered
out of what can
far and wide be seen,

shield against stimuli: consciousness,

cathexis-proof
me and also you,

hyperreal-
ized,
the eye-greedy, memory-
greedy, rolling
trade-
mark,

the temporal lobe intact,
like the sight stem.

AUS DEM MOORBODEN ins
Ohnebild steigen,
ein Häm
im Flintenlauf Hoffnung,
das Ziel, wie Ungeduld mündig,
darin.

Dorfluft, rue Tournefort.

TO CLIMB from quagmire into
the image want,
a haem
in the smoothbore of hope,
the mark, like impatience come
of age, within.

Village air, rue Tournefort.

HOCHMOOR, uhrglas-
förmig (einer hat Zeit),

soviel Ritter, sonnentausüchtig,

aus dem
Lagg
stehen die Sabbatkerzen nach oben,

Schwingmoor, wenn du vertorfst,
entzeigere ich
den Gerechten.

RAISED BOG, watchglass-
domed (there is one who has time),

so many swallowtails, hooked on sundew,

Sabbath candles, up-
standing in the
lagg,

quaking bog, when you turn to peat,
I shall undial
the righteous one.

ERZFLITTER, tief im
Aufruhr, Erzväter.

Du behilfst dir
damit,
als sprächen, mit ihnen,
Angiospermen
ein offenes
Wort.

Kalkspur Posaune.

Verlorenes findet
in den Karstwannen
Kargheit, Klarheit.

OREFLASHES, orefathers,
deep in the uproar.

You make of it
what you can,
as if angiosperms were
to speak with them
an open
word.

Chalkmark clarion.

In karst basins
what's lost finds
poverty, clarity.

EINKANTER: Rembrandt,
auf du und du mit dem Lichtschliff,
abgesonnen dem Stern
als Bartlocke, schläfig,

Handlinien queren die Stirn,
im Wüstengeschiebe, auf
den Tischfelsen
schimmert dir um den
rechten Mundwinkel der
sechzehnte Psalm.

ONE-FACED: Rembrandt,
thee and thou with the knap of light,
eclipsed from the star
as a lock of beard, the temple's,

palmlines score your brow,
in the desert till, on
pedestals of rock,
at the right hand
corner of your mouth
shimmers Psalm Sixteen.

MIT REBMESSERN, bei
Gebethub,
alle Marssegel spleißen,

herkämpfend, stehend, hinter
der Wimper, im Ölrock,
von Güssen gesalbt,

den Kalmengürtel schnüren
um deine Ulkspake, Beiboot
Welt.

WITH VINEHOOKS,
to splice all topsails
at prayer hoist,

advancing, standing, behind
the eyelash, in the robe of oil,
unctionbathed,

to wind the doldrums round
your toy capstan, quarterboat
world.

LÖSSPUPPEN: also
hier steints nicht,

nur Landschneckenhäuser,
unausgeblasen,
sagen zur Wüste: du
bist bevölkert –:

die Wildpferde stoßen
in Mammut-
hörner:

Petrarca
ist wieder
in Sicht.

LOESS DOLLS: no turning
to stone here,

just snailshells,
unblown,
telling the desert: you
are peopled –:

wild horses blast
on mammoth
horns:

Petrarch's
in sight
again.

V

STAHLSCHÜSSIGER SEHSTEIN, umstirnter,
dies hier:

die Palmfarne, jetzt,
in Castrup: ein
metallischer Vortrupp
des nächsten
Urjahrhunderts,

eine
Flughaut, lippig,
du
durchstößt sie,

die bildersüchtige blanke
Rolltreppe
kann dich nicht spiegeln.

STEELSHOT LENS-STONE, ringed by stars,
this here:

the palm ferns, now,
in Castrup: a
metallic outguard
of the next
ur-century,

a flying
membrane, lipped,
you
puncture it,

the image-craving blank
escalator
cannot mirror you.

UND KRAFT UND SCHMERZ
und was mich stieß
und trieb und hielt:

Hall-Schalt-
Jahre,

Fichtenrausch, einmal,

die wildernde Überzeugung,
daß dies anders zu sagen sei als
so.

AND FORCE AND PAIN
and what pressed and
drove and held me:

jubil-leapt
years,

the pinewood frenzy, once,

the unbridled conviction
this should be said other than
it is.

MITERHOBEN
von den Geräuschen,
forderst du – Glas
feindet an, was immer
undurchdringlicher dein ist –,
forderst du alles
in seine Aura,

das Quentchen Mut
bittert sich ein,
wachsam:
es weiß, daß du weißt.

UPLIFTED
by the commotion,
you summon – glass
abhors what's ever
more impenetrably yours –,
you summon everything
into its aura,

the dram of courage
bitters in,
watchful:
it knows that you know.

STEINSCHLAG hinter den Käfern.
Da sah ich einen, der log nicht,
heimstehn in seine Verzweiflung.

Wie deinem Einsamkeitssturm
glückt ihm die weit
ausschreitende Stille.

ROCKFALL, at the beetles' back.
I saw one there, who didn't lie,
stand the ground of his brokenness.

Happy – like your storm
of solitude – his far
carrying calm.

ICH SCHREITE deinen Verrat aus,
Fußspangen an
allen Seins-
gelenken,

Krümelgeister
kalben
aus deinen gläsernen
Titten,

mein Stein ist gekommen zu dir,
selbstentgittert, du inwendig
Ottern-
befrachtete,

du verhebst dich
an meinem leichtesten Schmerz,

du wirst sichtbar,

irgendein Toter, ganz bei sich,
setzt Lee über Luv.

I PACE out your betrayal,
fettered at every
joint
of my being,

spirit-shards
calve
from your cutglass
tits,

my stone is come to you
unbarred by its own devices, you,
in your inners
adder-freighted,

strain yourself
under the least of my sorrows,

you grow visible,

some dead man, come to himself,
sets lee over luff.

LEUCHTSTÄBE, deren
Gespräch,
auf Verkehrsinseln,
mit endlich beurlaubten
Wappen-Genüssen,

Bedeutungen
grätschen im aufgerissenen Pflaster,

das Küken
Zeit, putt, putt, putt,
schlüpft in den Kraken-Nerv,
zur Behandlung,

ein Saugarm holt sich
den Jutesack voller
Beschlußmurmeln aus
dem ZK,

die Düngerrinne herauf und herunter
kommt Evidenz.

FLASHLIGHTS, their
converse,
on traffic islands,
with armorial pleasures
finally paroled,

meanings
splay in the ripped-up cobbles,

chickling
time, putt–putt–putt,
slips into the kraken nerve
for nursing,

a suction arm extracts
the sack of mutter-
ed resolutions from
the ZK,

up and down the dung sewer
comes evidence.

EIN LESEAST, einer,
die Stirnhaut versorgend,

eine Lichtquelle, von dir
schläfrig geschluckt,
passiert das hungrige
Wirtsgewebe,

Sehhilfe, streifig,
über mondbefahrene
Rückstreu-Sonden. Im großen: im kleinen.

Erden, immer noch, Erden.
Hornhautüber-
zogner Basalt,
raketengeküßt:
kosmisches
Umlauf-Geschau, und doch:
Binnenland-Horizonte.

Terrestrisch, terrestrisch.

Ein Leseast, einer,
die Stirnhaut versorgend – als schriebst du
Gedichte –,
er trifft auf den Kartengruß auf,
damals, vorm
Blutklumpenort, auf der Lungen-
schwelle, jahrhin, aus Pilsen,
jahrüber,
zeitwild von soviel
Leisegepreßtem:

Bon vent, bonne mer,

A READING BRANCH, one that
innerves your brow skin,

a light source, swallowed
half in your sleep, passes
through the famished
host tissue,

visual assist, banded,
over moonswept
backscatter-probes. Macro: micro.

Earths, even now, earths.
Cornea-
coated basalt,
rocket-kissed:
a cosmic
seeing in the round, and yet:
inland horizons.

Terra, terra.

A reading branch, one that
innerves your brow skin – as if you wrote
poems –,
strikes on the postcard greeting,
back then, before the
bloodclot point, on the lungs'
threshold, down the year, from Pilsen,
through the year,
time-wild with so much quietly
express:

Bon vent, bonne mer,

ein flackernder
Hirnlappen, ein
Meerstück,

hißt, wo du lebst,
seine Hauptstadt, die
unbesetzbare.

a flapping lobe
of brain, a
strip of sea,
hoists, where you live,
its capital, not to
be seized.

ZERR DIR den Traum vom Stapel,
pack deinen Schuh rein,

Rauschelbeeräugige, komm,
schnür zu.

TEAR the dream from the bale,
pack your shoe in,

whinberry eyes, on
with the string.

KALK-KROKUS, im
Hellwerden: dein
steckbriefgereiftes
Von-dort-und-auch-dort-her,
unspaltbar,

Sprengstoffe
lächeln dir zu,
die Delle Dasein
hilft einer Flocke
aus sich heraus,

in den Fundgruben
staut sich die Moldau.

CHALK CROCUS, in
the breaking light: your
summons-ripened springing
from there and also there,
unfissile,

explosives
smile at you,
the hollow of being
helps a flake
to unflake,

the Moldau wells
in the lodeworks.

ES SIND SCHON die Kabel gelegt
zum Glück hinter dir
und zu dessen
munitionierten
Bereitstellungslinien,

in den Entlastungs-
städten,
dir zugewandt,
wo sie Gesundheitserreger versprühen,
melden melodische
Antitoxine
den Rennfahrerspurt
durch dein Gewissen.

THE CABLES are already laid
to the joy behind you
and to its
munitioned lines
of array,

in overspill
towns
turned to you,
under a shower of biogens,
melodic antitoxins
report the
overdrive
through your conscience.

IN DEN EINSTIEGLUKEN zur Wahrheit
beten die Spürgeräte,

bald kommen die Mauern geflogen
zu den Verhandlungstischen,

die Embleme palavern
sich Blut ab,

eine Krähe setzt
ihren halbgesichtigen
Peil-Flügel auf
halbmast.

IN THE ENTRY HATCHES to truth
the scanners are praying,

soon walls touch down at
conference tables,

the emblems jaw–jaw
blood,

a crow sets
its half-faced
compass wing to
half-mast.

UND JETZT, bei strategischer
Großlage, klauen-
signiertes
Gesinnungs-Lametta,

eine Wortlitze, rot-
gefüttert,
näht sich den Mündern
gesamtbarock in die
wund-
geschwiegene
Kommissur.

Schimmelbrothelle
eckt an,
abgekämpfte
Gedanken, was sonst,
stellen sich quer.

AND NOW, strategically
inleagued, conviction's
claw–
figured tinsel,

a red-lined word
braid
knits the mouths
baroquely of a piece
into the mute-
sore
commissure.

Breadmould light
elbows in,
battleweary thoughts,
what else, muster
a front.

SCHNELLFEUER-PERIHEL.

Reite dein Staubkorn zu,
ihr müßt mit,
mahnt das Flugblatt.

(Du, Akosmische, als ich.)

Eines Knödels Trabanten, klug,
auf den Geister-Pawlatschen.

QUICKFIRE PERIHELION.

The flysheet exhorts,
ride out your dustgrain,
you must go too.

(You, acosmic you, as I.)

Knödel satellites, canny,
round the spirit balconies.

WIR ÜBERTIEFTEN, geeinsamt
in der Gefrornis.
Jedes Hängetal karrt eine Wimper
an den Augenabdruck
und seinen Steinkern
heran.

WE THE OVERDEEPENED, set apart
in the permafrost.
Each hanging valley conducts a lash
to the eye's cast
and its fossil
core.

HINTER SCHLÄFENSPLITTERN,
im notfrischen
Holzwein,

(der Ort, wo du herkommst,
er redet sich finster, südwärts),

dahlienfürchtig bei Gold,
auf immer heiterern
Stühlen.

BEHIND TEMPLESPLINTERS,
in sorefresh
wood wine,

(the place you hail from
talks itself dark, bearing south),

pure-gold trembling before dahlias,
on seats ever
more serene.

BERGUNG allen
Abwässerglucksens
im Briefmarken-Unken-
ruf. Cor-
respondenz.

Euphorisierte
Zeitlupenchöre behirnter
Zukunftssaurier
heizen ein Selbstherz.

Dessen
Abstoß, ich wintre
zu dir über.

UMBRAGE of all
effluent belch
in the postage stamp croak-
ery. Cor-
respondence.

Euphoriate
slowmotion choirs of enbrained
future-age sauria
heat an idiot heart.

Whose
repulse I over-
winter to you.

DAS GEDUNKELTE Splitterecho,
hirnstrom-
hin,

die Buhne über die Windung,
auf die es zu stehn kommt,

soviel
Unverfenstertes dort,
sieh nur,

die Schütte
müßiger Andacht,
einen
Kolbenschlag von
den Gebetssilos weg,

einen und keinen.

THE DARKENED splinterecho
in the brainwave
current,

the buttress above the me-
ander where it is stayed,

so much
unwindowed there,
look,

the mow
of idle devotions,
one
rifle-butt from
the prayer silos,

one and none.

DIE EWIGKEIT hält sich in Grenzen:
leicht, in ihren
gewaltigen Meß-Tentakeln,
bedachtsam,
rotiert die von Finger-
nägeln durchleuchtbare
Blutzucker-Erbse.

ETERNITY holds within bounds:
weightless, in its
mighty tentacles of measure,
illuminable
by fingernails, the blood-
sugar pea, deliberate,
rotates.

GEDICHTE AUS DEM NACHLASS
(1968–1969)

OTHER POEMS
(1968–1969)

DAS GEISSBLATT BLÖKT:

eine neue Gemeinde
verheidet die Juden,

Leviten marschieren
durch meine Verdammung,
es tempelt
die wundgeschnittene
Pappel,

man sagt, die Zählenden
kannten mich nicht,
im Unterschied
zu –

THE GOAT'S-LEAF BLEATS:

a new communion
enheathens the Jews,

Levites march
through my damnation,
the gashed
poplar
temples,

they say, those counting
didn't know me,
un-
like –

DU,
du Vorgeprägte vom Feindstoß,
in dich ging ich,
in dir ging ich an,
was dich niederhielt,
auch den Abzähl-Haß,
aus dir hob ich
den Sohn,

gib ihn mir wieder,
du hast du auch dich

YOU,
stamped by the assault to come,
into you I went,
in you I came to be
the thing that held you down,
you and the hate of numbering off,
out of you I raised
the son,

give him me back,
you have, you too, you

SPRÜCHLEIN-DEUTSCH:
entdinglichte Welt, er–
fürchtet, erwirklicht,

Konstanze, heute,
wäre ein Tag,

Dora Dymant, heute,
ein Leben.

PROVERB-DEUTSCH:
unthinged world,
afeared, made real,

Konstanze, today,
were a day,

Dora Dymant, today,
a life.

PORT-BOU – DEUTSCH?

Pfeil die Tarnkappe weg, den
Stahlhelm.

Links-
nibelungen, Rechts-
nibelungen:
gerheinigt, gereinigt,
Abraum.

Benjamin
neint euch, für immer,
er jasagt.

Solcherlei Ewe, auch
als B-Bauhaus:
nein.

Kein Zu-spät,
ein geheimes
Offen.

PORT-BOU – DEUTSCH?

Arrow the cloak of invisibility, the
helmet of steel, into flight.

Nibelungs
on the left, Nibelungs
on the right:
purified, Rhenish'd,
dregs.

Benjamin
says no to you, forever,
the yeasayer.

Kindred eternals, even
unto B-Bauhaus:
no.

No Too-Late:
a secret
Open.

AM REIZORT. Stromstöße,
Impulse, grotesk,
doch alles.

Leitfähig jedes
eingeschlichene Amen,

aber wer hört
sein eigenes Ohr?

Schnürringe sinnen
dem offnen Quadrat nach:

denn es
menscht
die kontraktile
Monade.

STIMULUS POINT. Charges,
impulses, grotesque,
all told.

Conductive every
incrept amen,

but who hears
his own ear?

Constriction rings
ponder the open square:

the contractile
monad
becomes a
man.

OLDEST RED: eine Zahnvogelgegend.
Gesungen wird:
Wohin dein Woher?

Erhöhte
Denudation: Bekleidung, das ist:

Kleider, humid,
halten unhaus, versöhnen.

Die Trasse hat Ferien,

vorerkundet
gegenbreiig
jungsteints:

die Schleppungen
rennen,

Jehuda Halevi
singt den fränkischen Ritter
zustaub.

OLDEST RED: where birds are toothed.
It is sung:
where to your where from?

A higher
denuding: clothing, that is:

clothes, humid,
keep no-house, atone.

The routeline takes a break,

foreknowingly
unturbidly
neolithic:

the drag-folds
race,

Jehuda Halevi
sings to dust
the Frankish knight.

NACKTSAMER, hier dein
Gebetsmantel:
sprich dich
frei ins Geborgne.

Und gib dich mir zu
wie gewinnendes
Blau gewinnendem
Weiß.

GYMNOSPERM, here your
prayer mantle:
speak yourself
free into the mantled.

And give yourself
to me, like winning
blue to winning
white.

WIEVIELE,
die's nicht wissen in dieser Stadt,
in diesen Ländern und Städten?

Ihnen das Wissen,
das mitträgt am Kampf
gegen den mimigen
Terror.

Dein Stamm, der eine,
bäumt sich noch immer.

HOW MANY
who do not know in this town,
in these lands and towns?

Theirs the knowledge
that carries the fight
to mimic
terror.

Your line, alone, now
as then upreared.

ICH HÖRE SOVIEL VON EUCH,
daß ich nichts mehr höre
als Hören,

ich sehe soviel von euch,
daß ich nichts mehr sehe
als Sehen,

soviel rennt mich an
mit Gerede,
daß ich zuweilen spreche
wie einer, der redet,
daß ich zuweilen
spreche wie einer,
der schweigt.

Ich lebe, stark.

I HEAR SO MUCH OF YOU
that I hear nothing more
than hearing,

I see so much of you
that I see nothing more
than seeing,

so much assails me
with talk
that sometimes I speak
like one who talks,
sometimes I
speak like one
who is silent.

I live, strong.

DU BIST
OHNE ENDE.
Und niemand gewinnt,
was er nicht war, von dir her.

Friedliche Worte sagen:
du fielst
hinauf in den
Sieg.
Da stehst du, ein Stein, der
hat dich, wie er sich hat.

Ich weiß ja,
daß Du Mitwisser hast,
ich weiß auch:
Du überweißt sie
und Du erwählst.

Gleichewig mit Deiner Jugend
beginnst Du, gleichheutig.

YOU ARE
UNENDING.
And none wins
from you what he was not.

Words of peace say:
you fell
up into
victory.
There you stand, a stone, it
has you, as it has itself.

I know,
You have those who know with You,
I know also:
You outknow them
and You choose.

Coeternal with Your youth
You begin, as of today.

IN DEN SCHLAF, IN DEN STRAHL,
sie senden
Durchlicht:
kein Licht. Dein Aug sieht dein Auge: mehr.
Helligkeiten.

Und Israel, Land,
dich halt ich
herauf in das
Leben der Menschen,
der deinen,
die, unvollkommene, bürgen
für erstandenes Stehn, erfüllt,
für den Stoff,
der sich lebdenkt,
den Geist,
der sich denklebt.

INTO SLEEP, INTO THE BEAM,
they send
throughlight:
no light. Your eye sees your eye: more.
Luminosities.

And Israel, Land,
I lift you
up into the
life of men,
your own,
who, unended, stand bond
for a standing risen, borne,
for matter
that thinking lives,
spirit
that lives thinking.

In meinem zerschossenen Knie
stand mein Vater,

über-
sterbensgroß stand er
da,

Michailowka und
der Kirschgarten standen um ihn,

ich wußte, es würde
so kommen, sprach er.

In my shot knee stood
my father,

deathling
large
he stood there,

Michailowka and
the cherry garden stood round him,

I knew it
would come to this, he said.

Niemals, stehender Gram,
bist du vakant,

Vorgas-Träne, an dir
zerspellt die Granate,

da lacht
keiner,
und kein Mimetiker, noch so gelettert,
schrieb je ein Wort auf,
das rebelliert

Standing grief, at no time
are you vacant,

pre-gas tear, the grenade
spelts on you,

no one
laughs,
and no mime, however lettered,
wrote one word up
that rebels

IM UNAUFHELLBAREN
geht eine Tür,
von der
blättern die Tarnflecken ab,
die wahrheitsdurchnäßten.

WHERE NO LIGHT CAN BE SHED
is a door
shedding leaves
of camouflage
soaked through with truth.

LEB DIE LEBEN, leb sie alle,
halt die Träume auseinander,
sieh, ich steige, sieh, ich falle,
bin ein andrer, bin kein andrer.

LIVE THE LIVES, live them all,
tell the one dream from the other,
look, I rise, look, I fall,
am an other, am no other.

Du suchst Zuflucht
beim unauflöslichen
Erbstern – sie wird dir
gewährt. Jetzt
überlebst du dein zweites
Leben.

You seek asylum
with the indissoluble
ancestral star – it will be
given you. Now
you outlive your second
life.

Dir in die un-
gefalteten Hände
gewogen:
meiner Verzweiflung laut-
lose Geduld.

Weighed
into your un-
folded hands:
my despairing's noise-
less thole.

KEW GARDENS

Jetzt, wo
du dich häufst, wieder,
in meinen Händen,
abwärts im Jahr,

löst die angestammelte Meise
sich auf in lauter
Blau.

KEW GARDENS

Now, where
you amount, again,
in my hands,
bottomward in the year,

the stammered-at tit
dissolves in utter
blue.

Die Beschenkten
wollen
auch noch
bezahlt sein

Verkauft
von allen
wie jeder von uns
Wahr-
schreibenden

Bald ist morgen
und sagt:
auch ich
habe dich
verleugnet und bestohlen

In receipt
they
still want
paying

Sold out
by them all
like each of us
in truth
writing

Daybreak soon
with the words:
I too
have denied
and robbed you

Paul Celan

Celan was born Paul Antschel in Czernowitz, former capital of the autonomous Habsburg province of Bukovina, on 23 November 1920. His family belonged to a German-speaking Jewish community which had grown in strength and number over nearly 150 years of Austrian rule. The Versailles Treaty of 1919 assigned the region to Romania. In 1940, as a result of the Hitler-Stalin Pact, Czernowitz was occupied by the Red Army, and in the next year, with alliances reversed, by German and Romanian forces. In 1944 northern Bukovina, including Czernowitz, was annexed to the Ukraine, of which it remains part.

Having travelled to France as a medical student in 1938, Celan returned to Czernowitz in the summer of 1939 and took up the study of Romance languages and literatures. In 1942 his parents were deported to the Ukraine where, in the German Michailovka concentration camp, his father died of typhus and his mother was shot when no longer able to work. Their son survived the years 1942 to 1944 in a number of Moldavian labour camps. After the war Celan lived in Bucharest, working as a translator from Russian into Romanian, and, as a poet, adopting the anagram of his Romanian surname, Ancel. He escaped from Bucharest to Vienna in December 1947, and in 1948 issued his first collection of verse, *Der Sand aus den Urnen*, which he immediately withdrew because of printing errors. In the same year Celan settled in Paris, where he later married the graphic artist Gisèle de Lestrange, took French citizenship, and taught German literature at the École Normale Supérieure. In 1958 he was awarded the Bremen Literature Prize, and in 1960 the Georg Büchner Prize, the Federal Republic's highest literary award; the speeches which he made on each occasion are Celan's principal statements on his poetry. In April 1970 Paul Celan committed suicide by drowning in the Seine.

At his death, Celan had authorized the publication of seven volumes of verse: *Mohn und Gedächtnis* (1952), *Von Schwelle zu Schwelle* (1955), *Sprachgitter* (1959), *Die Niemandsrose* (1963), *Atemwende* (1967), *Fadensonnen* (1968), and *Lichtzwang* (1970). Since then, critical editions of these works have been supplemented by the issue of Celan's uncollected and unpublished poetry, prose, verse translations and correspondence.